The Loaf Cake Book

The best easy, tried and tested recipes all baked in a loaf tin

Barbara Glebska

THE LOAF CAKE BOOK
The best easy, tried and tested recipes all baked in a loaf tin

First Edition 2021

Copyright©2021Barbara Glebska
Photographs Copyright©2021Barbara Glebska
www.harrowphotographer.co.uk

No part of this publication may be reproduced, stored in a retrieval system or transmitted, in any form or by any means, electronic, mechanical, photocopying, recording or otherwise, without the prior written permission of the copyright holder.

CONTENTS

Almond and Orange Madeira Loaf
Banana, Chocolate Chip Tea Bread
Caramel Cake
Carrot, Pineapple and Walnut Loaf
Cherry and Chocolate Mousse Cake
Chocolate and Sour Cream Loaf
Chocolate Macaroon Loaf
Chocolate Marble Cake
Chocolate Chip and Orange Cake
Cinnamon and Sour Cream Crumble Cake
Coffee and Cream Cake
Fruit, Nut and Spice Cake
Lavender Cake
Layered Strawberry Cake
Lemon Layer Cake
Lime, Coconut and Ginger Cake
Marzipan and Cherry Cake
Orange and Vanilla Upside Down Cake
Peanut and Banana Cake
Pear and Cinnamon Cake
Pecan Cinnamon Swirl Loaf
Pistachio Cake
Plum and Custard Loaf Cake
Raspberry White Chocolate Cake
Red Velvet Cake
Sachertorte
Simnel Loaf Cake
Stem Ginger Cake
Toffee Apple Cake
Victoria Sponge

Hints and Tips

It is recommended using a digital scale for exact weight measurements which will result in consistent results and perfect cakes.

If you decide to use the cups volume method, fill the cup with the ingredient, then, scrape a knife across the top of the measuring cup to level the top.

• It is very important to follow the recipe at each stage and keep to the right oven temperatures. A few of the recipes ask that the temperature is lowered during baking, this ensures the cake is baked in the centre and doesn't sink.

• Set the oven rack to the middle of the oven

• Don't open the oven during the first 30 minutes of baking as the change in oven temperature might cause the cake to sink

• All the cakes are fully baked when a wooden skewer inserted into the middle of the cake comes out clean.

• Before starting a recipe prepare the tin and pre heat the oven.

• Have all the ingredients ready to hand.

• The cakes taste better the following day once completely cooled.

• The best way to line the tin is using parchment paper. This does not need any greasing. Line the tin with a strip of the paper with the ends overhanging the long sides of the tin. Loosen the end sides of the loaf cake with a knife when the cake is ready for taking out of the tin and pull up using the paper.

Tin size
All the recipes are calculated for a 900g/2lb tin Dimensions 14.5cm wide, 25cm long, 7cm tall (5 ¾ inches wide 10 inches long 2 ¾ inches tall).

Equipment
900g Loaf tin
Kitchen scales
Mixing bowl/s
Electric hand whisk or mixer
Measuring jug and spoons
Wooden spoons for mixing
Large metal spoon for folding in ingredients
Sieve
Wooden skewer

Conversion Tables

WEIGHT	VOLUME
25g - 1oz	1.25ml - ¼tsp
50g - 1¾oz	2.5ml - ½tsp
75g - 2¾oz	15ml - 1tsp
100g - 3½oz	30ml - 1fl oz
150g - 5½oz	50ml - 2fl oz
175g - 6oz	100ml - 3½fl oz
200g - 7oz	150ml - 5fl oz - ¼ pint
225g - 8oz	200ml - 7fl oz
250g - 9oz	300ml - 10 fl oz - ½ pint
275g - 9¾oz	500ml - 18fl oz
300g - 10½oz	600ml - 20fl oz - 1 pint
350g - 12oz	700ml - 1¼ pints
375g - 13oz	850ml - 1½ pints
400g - 14oz	1L - 1¾ pints
425g - 15oz	1.2L - 2 pints
450g - 1lb	
500g - 1lb 2oz	

Almond and Orange Madeira Loaf

Ingredients

265g (2 cups) plain flour
3 teaspoons baking powder
150g (1½ cups) ground almonds
250g (1¼ cups) caster sugar
½ teaspoon salt
5 medium eggs
300ml (1¼ cups) olive oil or rapeseed oil
2 oranges, juice and zest finely grated

Method

1. Preheat oven to 170°C / Gas 3 / 325°F
2. Line a 900g loaf tin with parchment paper.
3. Mix all the dry ingredients together then whisk in all the remaining ingredients till combined.
4. Spoon the mixture into the tin and bake for 1 hour and 20 minutes until a skewer inserted into the cake comes out clean.
5. Leave to cool in the tin. then transfer to a plate.

Banana, Chocolate Chip Tea Bread

Ingredients

2 Eggs
150ml (¾ cup) Vegetable Oil
225g (1 cup) Caster Sugar

4 Bananas
60g (2/3 cup) Rolled Oats
300g (2½ cup) Plain Flour
1 teaspoon Baking Powder
1 teaspoon Bicarbonate soda
2 teaspoons Ground Cinnamon
100g (¾ cup) Dark Chocolate chopped into chunks

Method

1. Preheat the oven to 180°C / gas 4 / 350°F
2. Line a 900g loaf tin with parchment paper
3. Whisk the eggs, oil, and sugar together until thick
4. Slice the bananas thinly and whisk into the mixture so that they break up
5. Fold in all the remaining ingredients until the mixture is smooth
6. Pour the batter into the prepared tin
7. Bake on a middle shelf of the oven for 30 minutes then reduce the temperature to 150°C / Gas 2 / 300°F for 60 minutes
8. The cake is done when a skewer inserted into the middle of the cake comes out clean.
9. Allow the cake to cool in the tin then transfer to a plate.

NOTE: The chocolate can be substituted for 100g dried fruit

Caramel Cake

Ingredients

265g (1¼ cup) butter, softened
180g (1 cup) light brown muscovado sugar
300g (1¼ cup) Nestle Carnation Caramel
300g (2½ cups) self-raising flour
4 large eggs
2 teaspoons caramel flavouring (optional)

Icing
75g (1/3 cup) butter
75g (1/3 cup) light brown muscovado sugar
2tbsp Nestle Carnation Caramel
1 teaspoon caramel flavouring
40g (1/3 cup) icing sugar

Method

1. Preheat the oven to 180°C / gas 4 / 350°F
2. Line a 900g loaf tin with parchment paper.
3. Place all the cake ingredients in a large bowl and use an electic whisk to beat together until all the ingredients are combined.
4. Tip the mixture into the cake tin.
5. Bake for 45 minutes then reduce the oven to 150°C / Gas 2 / 300°F and bake for a further 10 minutes till a skewer inserted in the centre come out clean.
6. Leave to cool in the tin then turn out on to a plate.

Icing
Melt together the butter, sugar, caramel and flavouring in a pan until smooth, stirring. Remove from the heat, sift in the icing sugar and mix together.
Cool until lukewarm then spoon and spread over the cake. Leave to set.

Carrot, Pineapple and Walnut Loaf

Ingredients

250g (2 cups) self-raising flour
¼ teaspoon baking powder
¼ teaspoon bicarbonate of soda
½ teaspoon ground cinnamon
¼ teaspoon freshly grated nutmeg
¼ teaspoon salt

4 medium eggs
200ml vegetable oil
2 tablespoons hot water
250g (1¼ cup) caster sugar

175g (2 cups) carrots, peeled and grated
90g (1 cup) chopped walnuts
120g (½ cup) fresh or tinned pineapple, diced 1cm pieces

Topping

100g (½ cup) cube butter, (not spread) softened
100g (3/4 cup) icing sugar
½ tsp vanilla extract
200g (1 cup) cream cheese, drained

3 tablespoons grated white chocolate (optional)

Method

1. Preheat the oven to 170°C / gas 3 / 325°F
2. Line a 900g loaf tin with parchment paper.
3. Sieve the flour, baking powder, bicarbonate of soda, spices and salt into a large bowl.
4. Whisk the oil and eggs together lightly. in a jug.
5. Add to the dry ingredients and mix well.
6. Stir in the hot water then the sugar.
7. Fold in the carrots, walnuts and pineapple.
8. Spoon into the tin. Bake for 1 hour, then reduce to 150°C / Gas 2 / 300°F for 20minutes or until a skewer comes out clean.
9. Leave to cool in the tin.

Topping

1. Beat the butter and sugar together till smooth, add the vanilla, then beat in the cream cheese. Spread over the cold cake.
2. Sprinkle with the white chocolate, if using, and serve.

Cherry and Chocolate Mousse Cake

Ingredients

100g (¾ cup) dark chocolate
200g (approximately 30 fingers) pack Sponge fingers
175ml (¾ cup) red or white grape juice
300ml (1¼ cup) whipping cream or double cream or a mix of the two
300g (2 cups) fresh cherries, stoned and halved
55g (3/4 cup) roasted flaked almonds

Decoration (optional) eg. extra cherries, grated chocolate, whipped cream

Method

1. Melt the chocolate in a basin over a pan of simering water. Leave to cool for 15 minutes
2. Line a 900g loaf tin with cling film
3. Dip the sponge fingers in the juice and line the base and sides of the tin
4. Whip the creams together till stiff
5. Mix the cooled chocolate into the cream, followed by the cherries and almonds
6. Fill the sponge lined tin with the chocolate mixture
7. Cover with more sponge fingers dipped in juice
8. Cover with cling film and refrigerate for at least 8 hours
9. Turn the cake out on to a serving plate and decorate to your liking.

Chocolate & Soured Cream Loaf

Ingredients

260g (1¼ cup) salted butter
230g (1½ cup) dark chocolate, chopped into small chunks
135g (3/4 cup) caster sugar
100g (½ cup) light brown soft sugar

5 medium eggs
1½ teaspoon vanilla extract
115g (½ cup) soured cream
3tbs milk

225g (2 cups) plain flour
35g (¼ cup) cocoa powder
1½ teaspoon baking powder
1 teaspoon bicarbonate of soda

Topping
50g (¼ cup) dark chocolate, chopped
50g (¼ cup) soured cream
1 tablespoon caster sugar

Method

1. Preheat the oven to 180°C / gas 4 / 350°F
2. Line a 900g loaf tin with baking parchment.
3. Place the butter, 115g (half) the chopped chocolate and both sugars in a medium saucepan and set over a low heat, stirring until melted. Set aside to cool.
4. Whisk the eggs, vanilla, soured cream and milk in a separate bowl.
5. Combine the remaining dry ingredients in another bowl.
6. Whisk the cooled chocolate mixture into the egg mixture until combined.
7. Then sift in the dry ingredients and whisk gently until mixed.
8. Stir through the remaining 115g chopped chocolate, then tip into the tin.
9. Bake for 30 minutes until risen and then reduce the oven temperature to 150°C / Gas 2 / 300°F for 50 minutes until a skewer inserted into the centre comes out clean.
10. Cool in the tin for 15 minutes, then remove onto a wire rack.

Topping
1. Heat all the topping ingredients in a heatproof bowl set over a pan of gently simmering water. Stir occasionally until melted and combined.
2. Stir in 1 tbsp just-boiled water until glossy, then spread over the cooled cake and allow to cool and set before slicing.

Chocolate Macaroon Loaf

Ingredients

Filling

2 egg whites, reserving the yolks
110g (½ cup) caster sugar
2 tablespoons plain flour
1 teaspoon vanilla essence
110g (¼ cup) desiccated coconut
170g (1 cup) chocolate chips

Cake ingredients

230g (2 cups) plain flour
275g (1½ cup) caster sugar
50g (½ cup) cocoa powder
½ teaspoon salt
1 tsp baking soda
2 teaspoons vanilla
3 eggs
2 reserved egg yolks
100ml (1/3 cup) milk
110g (½ cup) butter, softened
110ml (1/3 cup) sour cream

Method

Filling

1. Preheat the oven to 180°C / gas 4 / 350°F and put a baking tray on the middle shelf.
2. Line a 900g loaf tin with baking parchment.
3. In a small bowl beat the egg whites until foamy.
4. Gradually beat in the 110g sugar until stiff.
5. Fold in the rest of the filling ingredients.

Cake

1. In a separate large bowl place all the cake ingredients and and beat till well combined.
2. Spoon one third of the cake batter into the prepared tin. Drop half the coconut filling in the centre of the batter to form a long strip lenthways. Keeping it away from the long sides of the tin
3. Cover filling with one third of the remaining batter and repeat with the remaining filling. Cover with the rest of the batter.
4. Place on the baking tray in the oven and bake for 50 minutes, then reduce oven to 150°C / Gas 2 / 300°F for 25 minutes.
5. Remove from the oven and allow to cool before taking out of the tin.

Chocolate Marble Cake

Ingredients

200g (1 3/4 cups) self-raising flour
1 teaspoon baking powder
80g (½ cup) plain chocolate, broken into pieces
250g (1 cup) unsalted butter
220g (1 cup) caster sugar
4 medium eggs
1 tsp vanilla essence
3 tablespoons milk
60g (½ cup) ground almonds

For the icing
60g (½ cup) plain chocolate, broken into pieces
30g (¼ cup) unsalted butter

Method

1. Preheat the oven to 180°C / gas 4 / 350°F
2. Line a 900g loaf tin with parchment paper
3. Sift the flour with the baking powder and a pinch of salt.
4. Melt the chocolate over a pan of gently simmering water, or in the microwave.
5. Cream the butter and the sugar until light and fluffy.
6. Beat in 2 eggs, the vanilla essence and half the flour and milk. Repeat with the rest of the eggs and flour.
7. Fold in the ground almonds.
8. Put half the batter in a separate bowl and stir in the melted chocolate. Now drop alternating spoonfuls of the two mixtures into the tin.
9. Draw a knife through the duo of mixes, swirling them into marbled patterns.
10. Bake for 50 - 55 minutes. Test by plunging a skewer into the centre – if it comes out clean, it's ready. Let the cake cool in the tin then turn out onto a plate.

Icing
Melt the chocolate with the butter in a pan over simmering water, or in the microwave. Stir, and spoon over the cake.

Chocolate Chip and Orange Cake

Ingredients

200g (1 cup) butter
200g (1 cup) caster sugar
2 eggs
284ml soured cream
300g (2½ cup) plain flour
1 teaspoon bicarbonate of soda
1 teaspoon baking powder
pinch salt
200g (1¼ cup) milk chocolate, roughly chopped
2 oranges, zest
1 teaspoon orange flavouring (optional)

Method

1. Preheat the oven to 180°C / gas 4 / 350°F
2. Line a 900g loaf tin with parchment paper
3. Cream the butter and sugar until pale and fluffy
4. Add the eggs one at a time and beat until incorporated
5. Using a wooden spoon stir in half the soured cream
6. Sift the dry ingredients and add to the mixture
7. Then fold in the remaining soured cream
8. Fold the chocolate, orange zest and flavouring through the mixture
9. Bake for 50 mins then reduce the oven to 150°C / Gas 2 / 300°F and bake for another 30-35 mins till a skewer inseted into the middle comes out clean
10. Leave to cool in the tin.

Cinnamon and Sour Cream Crumble Cake

Ingredients

Crumble
100g (½ cup) light brown sugar
95g (3/4 cup) plain flour
2 teaspoons ground cinnamon
65g (¼ cup) unsalted butter, cold and cubed

Cake
170g (3/4 cup) unsalted butter
200g (1 cup) caster sugar
3 large eggs
3 teaspoons vanilla extract
200ml full-fat sour cream
250g (2 cups) plain flour
1½ teaspoon baking powder
½ teaspoon baking soda
¼ teaspoon salt

Method

Crumble
Place all the crumble ingredients in a bowl and rub together with finger tips to combine until the mixture resembles pea sized crumbs. Set aside.

Cake
1. Preheat oven to 170°C / Gas 3 / 325°F
2. Line a 900g loaf tin with parchment paper.
3. Beat the butter and the sugar a until creamed together.
4. Add 1 egg at a time, beating well after each addition.
5. Beat in the vanilla extract and sour cream.
6. Beat in all the dry ingredients until just combined. Do not overmix this batter. The batter will be smooth and thick.
7. Carefully spread half of the batter into the pan. Sprinkle with half of the crumble.
8. Spread the remaining half of the batter on top, then the remaining crumble
9. Bake for 1 hour or until the cake is baked through. To test, insert a skewer into the center of the cake. If it comes out clean, it is done. Allow cake to cool in the pan before turning out on a plate.

Coffee and Cream Cake

Ingredients

300g (2½ cup) self raising flour
1 teaspoon baking powder
200g (1¼ cup) light brown sugar
½ teaspoon nutmeg
pinch of salt

1 tablespoon instant coffee powder
250g (1 cup) unsalted Butter, melted
75ml milk
175g (1 cup) fresh vanilla custard
3 medium eggs

Syrup
1 teaspoon instant coffee powder
3 tablespoon caster sugar

Topping
2 tablespoons caster sugar
200ml double cream
100g (½ cup) fresh vanilla custard

Cocoa for dusting

Method

1. Preheat the oven to 180°C / gas 4 / 350°F
2. Line a 900g loaf tin with parchment paper
3. In a large bowl mix together the flour, baking powder, light brown sugar, nutmeg, and salt.
4. In a cup mix 1 tablespoon coffee with 1 tablespoon hot water and stir into the melted butter along with the milk, custard and eggs.
5. Whisk the wet ingredients into the flour mixture.
6. Pour into the tin and bake for 1 hour or until a skewer inseted into the cake comes out clean.
7. Allow the cake to cool in it's tin.

Syrup
1. Mix 1 teaspoon coffee with 3 tablespoons caster sugar and 1 tablespoon hot water to make a syrup.
2. Poke holes all over the cake and brush with the coffee syrup.
3. Once cooled completely remove from the tin and slice into 3 layers.

Topping
1. Make the topping by whipping the cream with the 2 tablespoons sugar until very thick then fold in the 100g custard.
2. Spoon 1/3 of the cream on each layer finishing with the top of the cake.
3. Dust with cocoa powder.

Fruit, Nut and Spice Cake

Ingredients

225g (1 cup) salted Butter
225g (1 cup) light muscovado sugar
1 teaspoon mixed spice
1 teaspoon ground nutmeg
3 medium eggs
350g (3 cups) self raising flour
100g (1 cup) ground almonds
200g (1¼ cup) mixed dried fruit
100g (½ cup) glace cherries
50g (½ cup) chopped walnuts
150ml milk

Method

1. Preheat the oven to 170°C / gas 3 / 325°F
2. Line a 900g loaf tin with parchment paper
3. Beat together the butter, sugar, and spices until pale and creamy
4. Gradually beat in the eggs, adding a spoonful of flour if the mixture starts to curdle.
5. Stir in the flour and almonds
6. Add the dried fruit, cherries and walnuts.
7. Finally stir in the milk.
8. Turn into the tin and level the surface
9. Bake for 1.5 hours or until a skewer inserted into the centre comes out clean.
10. Leave to cool in the tin.

Lavender Cake

Ingredients

200g (1 3/4 cups) Self raising flour
1 teaspoon Baking Powder
Pinch of salt

250g (1 cup) unsalted butter
200g (1 cup) caster sugar
4 eggs
3 tablespoons milk
60g (½ cup) ground almonds
2 tablespoons dried lavender or fresh lavender flowers and leaves

Lavender Lemon Glaze
3 tablespoons lemon juice
2 teaspoons dried lavender or 3 teaspoons fresh lavender flowers
150g (1 ¼ cup) Icing sugar

Lavender flowers to decorate (optional)

Method

1. Preheat the oven to 180°C / gas 4 / 350°F
2. Line a 900g loaf tin with parchment paper
3. Sift flour, baking powder and a pinch of salt
4. In a separate bowl cream the butter and sugar until light and fluffy
5. Beat in two eggs, then half the flour and 2 tablespoons milk. Repeat then fold in the ground almonds and lavender.
6. Add enough milk to give a thick dropping consistency
7. Bake for 40 mins on gas 4 then reduce to 150°C / Gas 2 / 300°F for 25 minutes until firm to the touch.
8. Test by plunging a skewer into the centre - if it comes out clean, it's ready.
9. Leave to cool in the tin then take out onto a plate.

Lavender Lemon Glaze
Poke some small holes around the top of the cake with skewer to allow the glaze to fully absorb.

1. Combine the lemon juice and lavender in a small saucepan, bring to a boil, remove and let steep for 5 minutes.
2. Mix in the icing sugar till smooth
3. Pour the glaze over the cake and let the cake sit for at least 1 hour before serving.

Layered Strawberry Cake

Ingredients

125g (½ cup) unsalted butter, softened,
180g (1 cup) caster sugar
4 medium eggs, lightly beaten
190g (1½ cup) self-raising flour
4 tablespoons whole milk
2 teaspoons vanilla essence

Filling
600ml double cream
2 tablespoons caster sugar
1 teaspoon vanilla essence
400g (2 cups) fresh strawberries sliced

Method

1. Preheat the oven to 180°C / gas 4 / 350°F
2. Line a 900g loaf tin with parchment paper
3. In a bowl, use an electric beater to cream together the butter and sugar until pale and fluffy.
4. Beat in the eggs, then sift in the flour and mix well to combine.
5. Stir in the milk and vanilla.
6. Spoon the mixture into the prepared loaf tin and bake for 30 minutes then reduce the oven to 150°C / Gas 2 / 300°F and bake for a further 25 minutes until a skewer inserted into the centre of the cake comes out clean.
7. Carefully lift out of the tin and leave to cool on a wire rack.
8. When the cake is cooled completely, cut it horizontally into 3 layers.

Filling
1. Whisk together the cream, vanilla essence and sugar.
2. Spread the cream equally between each of the layers, topping each layer with the sliced strawberries.

Cook's tip
Use a serrated knife to slice cleanly through the cake for neat servings

Lemon Layer Cake

Ingredients

225g (2 cups) self-raising flour
2 teaspoons baking powder
225g (1 cup) soft butter
220g (1 cup) caster sugar
4 large eggs
1 lemon, juice and grated zest

Filling

200g (1 cup) full fat cream cheese (drained)
2tbsp icing sugar
100g (1/3 cup) lemon curd

Method

1. Preheat the oven to 180°C / gas 4 / 350°F
2. Line a 900g loaf tin with parchment paper
3. Place all the cake ingredients in a large bowl and whisk to combine until smooth.
4. Pour the mixture into the tin and bake for 30 minutes. Reduce the oven to 150°C / Gas 2 / 300°F and bake for a further 30 minutes or until a skewer inserted in the centre of the cake comes out clean.
Leave the cake to cool in the tin.

Filling

1. In a bowl combine the cheese and sieved icing sugar
2. Ripple the lemon curd through the mixture.
3. Cut the cake horizontally to give 3 layers.
Use the lemon curd mixture to sandwich the cake together and dust lightly with icing sugar.

Lime, Coconut and Ginger Cake

Ingredients

265g (1¼ cup) unsalted butter
265g (1¼ cup) caster sugar
5 medium eggs
190g (1½ cup) plain flour
115g (1¼ cup) desiccated coconut
2 teaspoons baking powder
5 balls stem ginger finely chopped plus 3 tablespoons ginger syrup
225ml unsweetened lime juice (or juice from 7 limes)
150g (1¼ cup) icing sugar

Zest strands from 1 lime (optional for decoration)

NOTE: The cake should be left at least 12 hours to allow for the lime juice to be absorbed before eating.

Method

1. Preheat the oven to 180°C / gas 4 / 350°F
2. Line a 900g loaf tin with parchment paper
3. Beat the butter and sugar together until light and fluffy.
4. Gradually add the eggs with a little flour and beat well.
5. Fold in the remaining flour along with the coconut, baking powder, stem ginger, stem ginger syrup, 3 tablespoons lime juice and a pinch of salt.
6. Spoon the mixture into the loaf tin levelling out the top.
7. Bake for 30mins on the middle oven shelf then reduce the oven to 150°C / Gas 2 / 300°F for 55 mins until golden and a skewer inserted into the cake comes out clean.
8. Set aside 3 tablespoons lime juice – mix the remainder with 1 tablespoon icing sugar.
9. When the cake is baked prick the top with a skewer and pour over the drizzle.
10. Leave to cool in the tin then take out onto a plate.
11. When cool, sift the remaining icing sugar into a bowl stir in the reserved 3 tbsp lime juice to form a thick icing.
12. Spread over the cake allowing some to run down the sides.
13. Decorate with strands of lime zest.

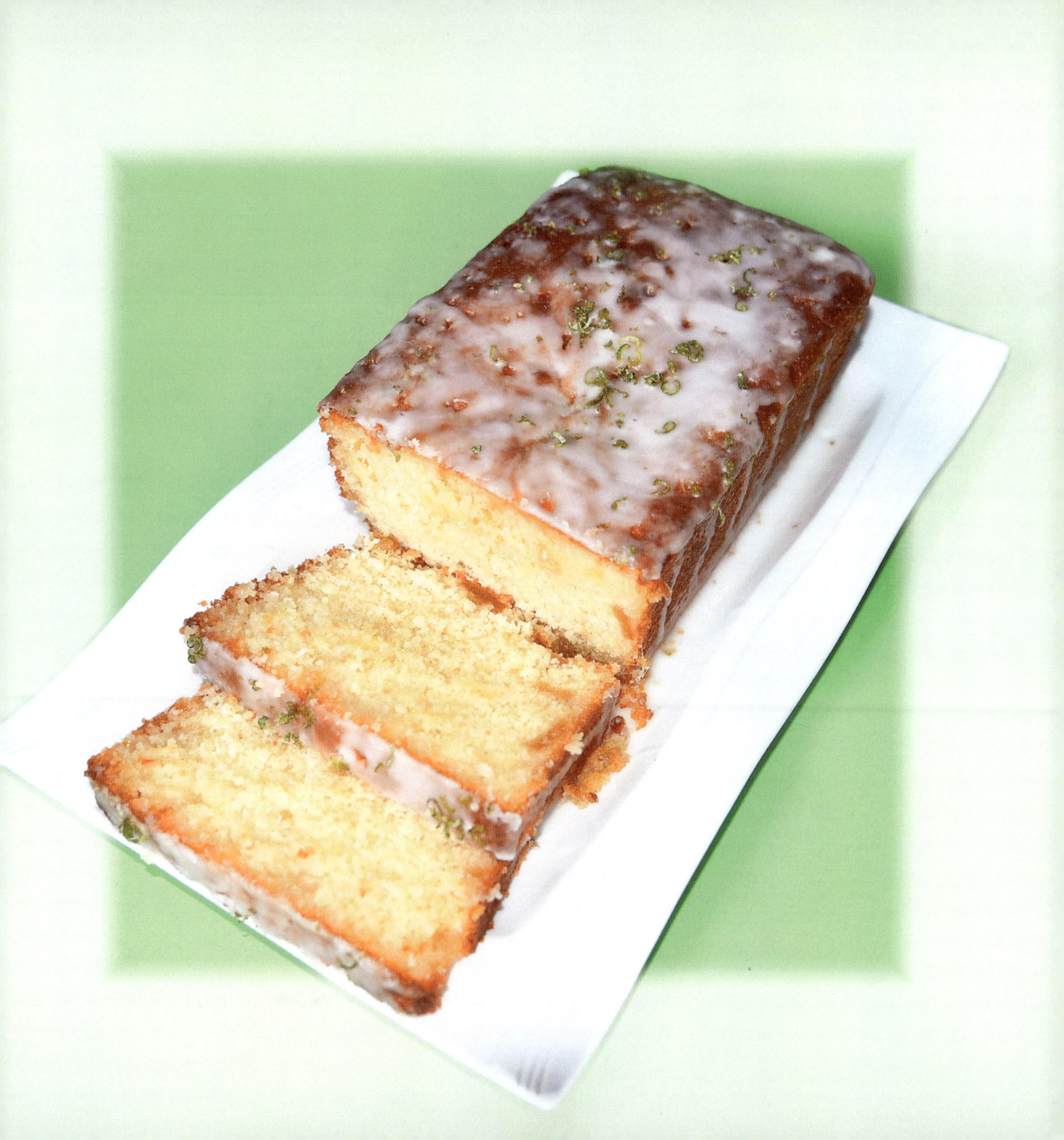

Marzipan and Cherry Cake

Ingredients

200g (¾ cup) marzipan (almond paste) cut into 1cm cubes
200g (1 cup) glace cherries, halved
200g (1 cup) unsalted butter
150g (¾ cup) caster sugar
3 large eggs
1 teaspoon vanilla extract
1 teaspoon almond extract
150g (1¼ cup) self-raising flour, plus 2 tablespoons
80g (3/4 cup) ground almonds
2 tablespoons lemon juice

Method

1. Preheat the oven to 170°C / gas 3 / 325°F
2. Line a 900g loaf tin with parchment paper
3. Toss the marzipan and cherries in 2 tablespoons flour and set aside
4. Beat the butter and sugar together until light and fluffy
5. Gradually add the eggs one at a time beating between additions
6. Add the vanilla and almond extracts
7. Then fold in the flour and ground almonds followed by the lemon juice
8. Spoon 2/3 of the batter into the tin
9. Top with half the cherries and marzipan
10. Cover with the remaining batter and top with the remaining cherries and marzipan pressing them down slightly
11. Bake for 1 hour 15 minutes covering losely with foil if the cake browns too quickly.
12. Check that a skewer comes out clean before taking out of the oven and leaving to cool in the tin.

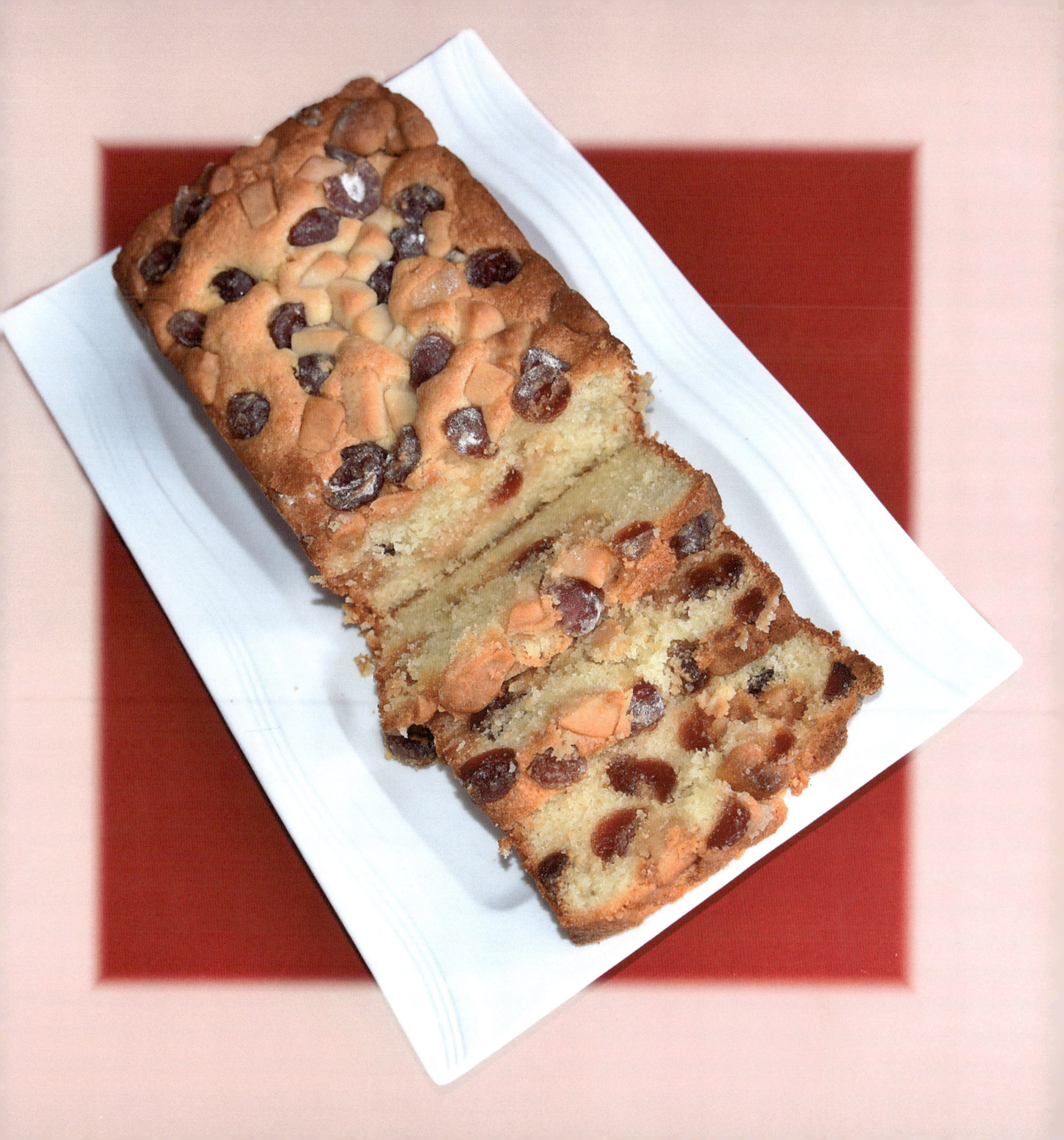

Orange and Vanilla Upside-down Cake

Ingredients

4 eggs
175g (1 cup) caster sugar
1 teaspoon vanilla extract
150g (1¼ cup) self-raising flour
150g (¾ cup) butter, melted
120g (1 cup) ground almonds

Topping
220g (1 cup) caster sugar
125ml water
1 teaspoon vanilla extract
2 oranges, very thinly sliced (½ cm thick)

Method

1. Put a baking tray on the middle shelf of the oven and preheat to 170°C / gas 3 / 325°F
2. Line a 900g loaf tin with parchment paper

Topping
1. Place the sugar, water and vanilla in a 20cm frying pan over medium heat. Stir until the sugar is dissolved.
2. Add the sliced oranges and simmer for 10-15 minutes or until the orange is soft. Remove from the heat and set aside.
3. When the oranges have cooled slightly, arrange them in the bottom and up the sides of the tin.
4. Pour in 100ml of the left over sugar syrup into the tin over the oranges. Reserve the rest.

Cake
1. Place eggs, sugar and vanilla in a bowl and whisk until the mixture is thick and tripled in volume.
2. Sift the flour over the egg mixture and fold through.
3. Fold through the melted butter and ground almonds
4. Pour the mixture over the oranges and bake for 60 minutes or until a skewer inserted in the cake comes out clean.
5. Prick the cake with a skewer and drizzle with 6 tablespoons of the reserved syrup.
6. Leave to cool then turn out upside down onto a platter to serve.

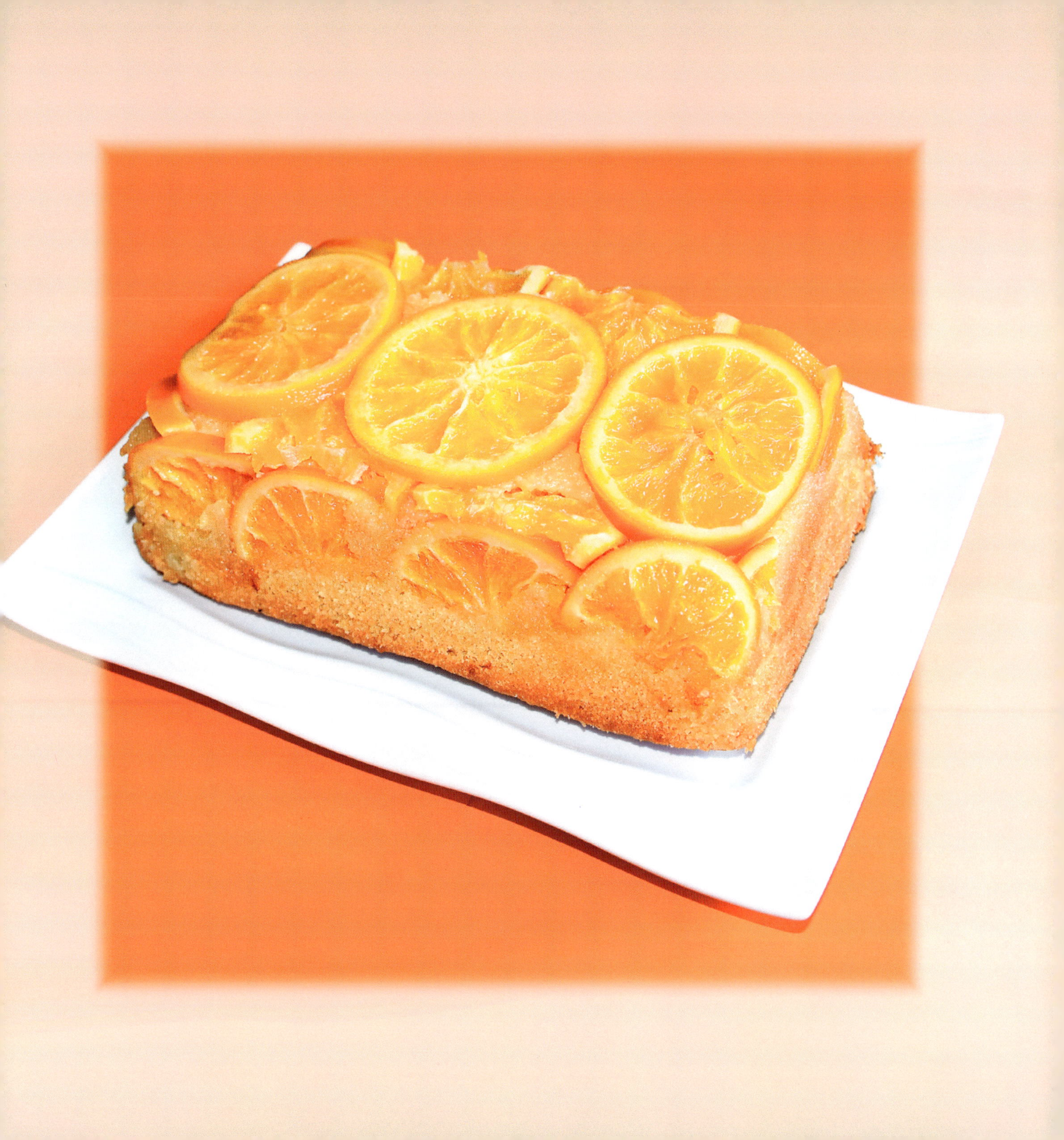

Peanut and Banana Cake

Ingredients

150g (¾ cup) butter
150g (¾ cup) Light Brown Soft Sugar
85g (¼ cup) Smooth Peanut Butter
2 large eggs
1 teaspoon vanilla extract
3 bananas
300g (2½ cup) self raising flour
1 teaspoon baking powder

Topping

35g (¼ cup) unsalted butter
115g (1 cup) icing sugar
60g (¼ cup) smooth peanut butter
60g (¼ cup) full fat soft cheese (drained)
30g (¼ cup) roasted salted peanuts chopped

Method

1. Preheat the oven to 180°C / gas 4 / 350°F
2. Line a 900g loaf tin with parchment paper
3. Cream the butter and sugar until fluffy
4. Beat in the peanut butter, then the eggs and vanilla.
5. Cut the bananas into thin slices and whisk into the mixture so that they break up and combine.
6. Fold in the flour and baking powder.
7. Bake for 50 mins in the tin until a skewer put into the centre comes out clean.
8. Cool completely in the tin.

Topping

1. Beat the butter until creamy then beat in the sieved icing sugar until crumbly
2. Beat in the peanut butter followed by the cheese to make a spreadable icing (do not overbeat)
3. Ice the cake then sprinkle with the peanuts.

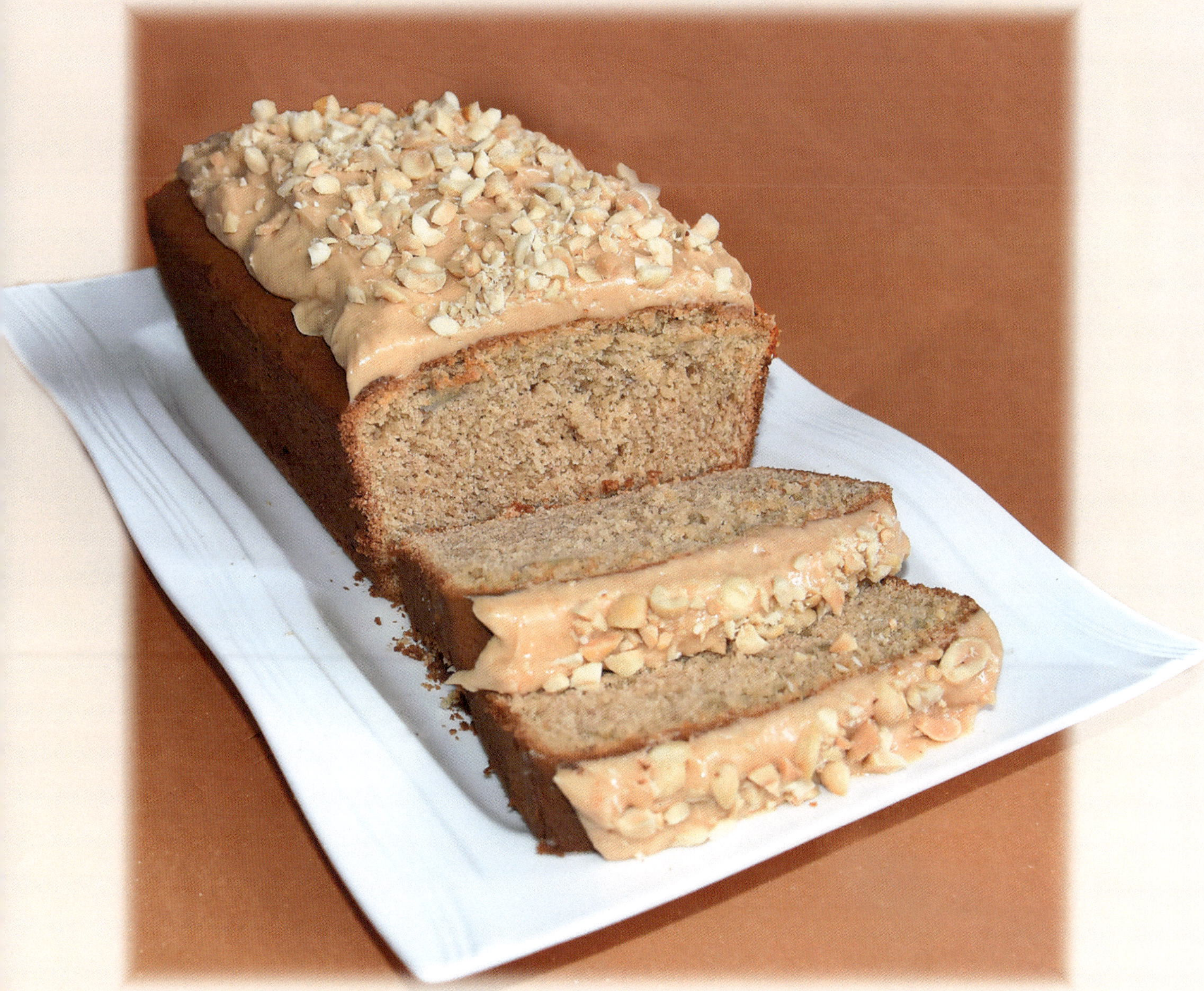

Pear and Cinnamon Cake

Ingredients

175g (¾ cup) salted butter
150g (¾ cup) light brown sugar
3 medium eggs
150g (1¼ cup) self raising flour
100g (1 cup) ground almonds
1 teaspoon ground cinnamon
4 Conference pears, peeled, cored and cut into 1cm chunks

Topping
1 tablespoon demerara sugar
2 tablespoon flaked almonds

Method

1. Preheat the oven to 170°C / gas 3 / 325°F
2. Line a 900g/2lb loaf tin with baking parchment
3. Using electric beaters cream the butter and sugar until light and fluffy.
4. Beat in the eggs one at a time
5. Mix the flour, almonds, and cinnamon in a bowl then beat into the butter to combine.
6. Pour half the mixture into the prepared tin then scatter with half the pears. Cover with the remaining mixture then scatter the remaining pears on top.
7. Scatter the demerara sugar on top of the cake followed by the flaked almonds.
8. Bake for 1 hour 30 minutes until a skewer inserted into the cake comes out clean.
9. Leave to cool in the tin before taking out onto a plate.

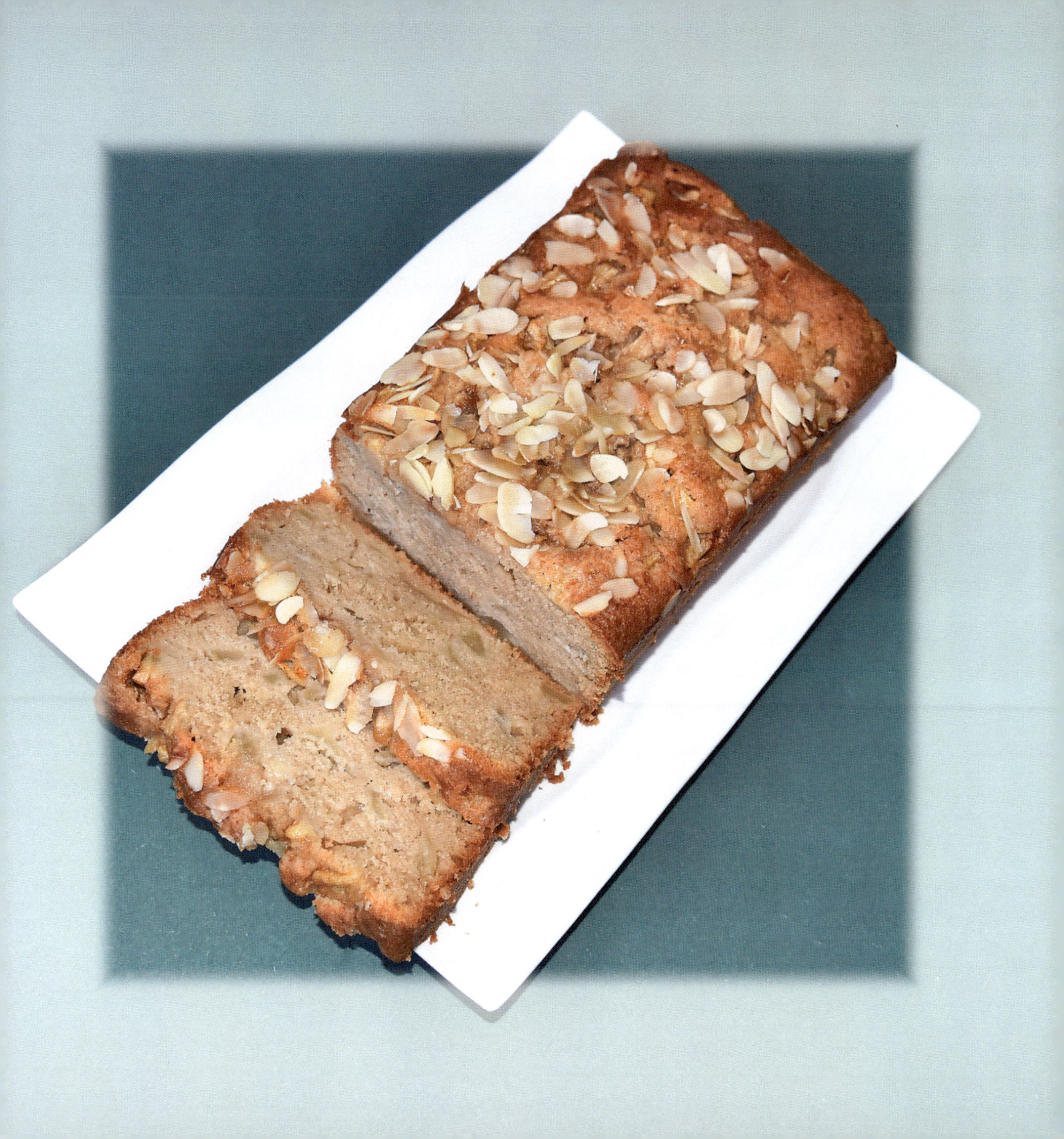

Pecan Cinnamon Swirl Loaf

Ingredients

225g (1 cup) salted butter
200g (1 cup) caster sugar
4 large eggs
1 tablespoon vanilla extract
250ml milk
450g (3½ cup) plain flour
2 teaspoons baking powder

Brown Sugar Filling

180g (¾ cup) brown sugar
120g (1 cup) chopped pecans
120g (½ cup) butter, softened
2 tablespoons all-purpose flour
2 tablespoons ground cinnamon

Method

1. Preheat the oven to 180°C / gas 4 / 350°F
2. Line a 900g loaf tin with parchment paper, hanging the edges over the sides.
3. In a small bowl, mix together all the brown sugar filling ingredients; set aside.
4. In a large mixing bowl, beat together the butter and sugar until fluffy. Beat in eggs, vanilla, and milk.
5. Add the flour and baking powder mixing until just smooth.
6. Pour half the batter into the prepared loaf tin, top with ¾ of the brown sugar filling, then remaining batter, then remaining filling.
7. Using a knife, swirl the batter to create a marbled effect.
8. Bake for 35 minutes then reduce oven to 150°C / Gas 2 / 300°F and bake for an extra 60 minutes until a skewer inserted in the centre comes out clean.
9. Let loaf cool for 1 hour in the loaf pan, then transfer to a wire rack to cool completely.

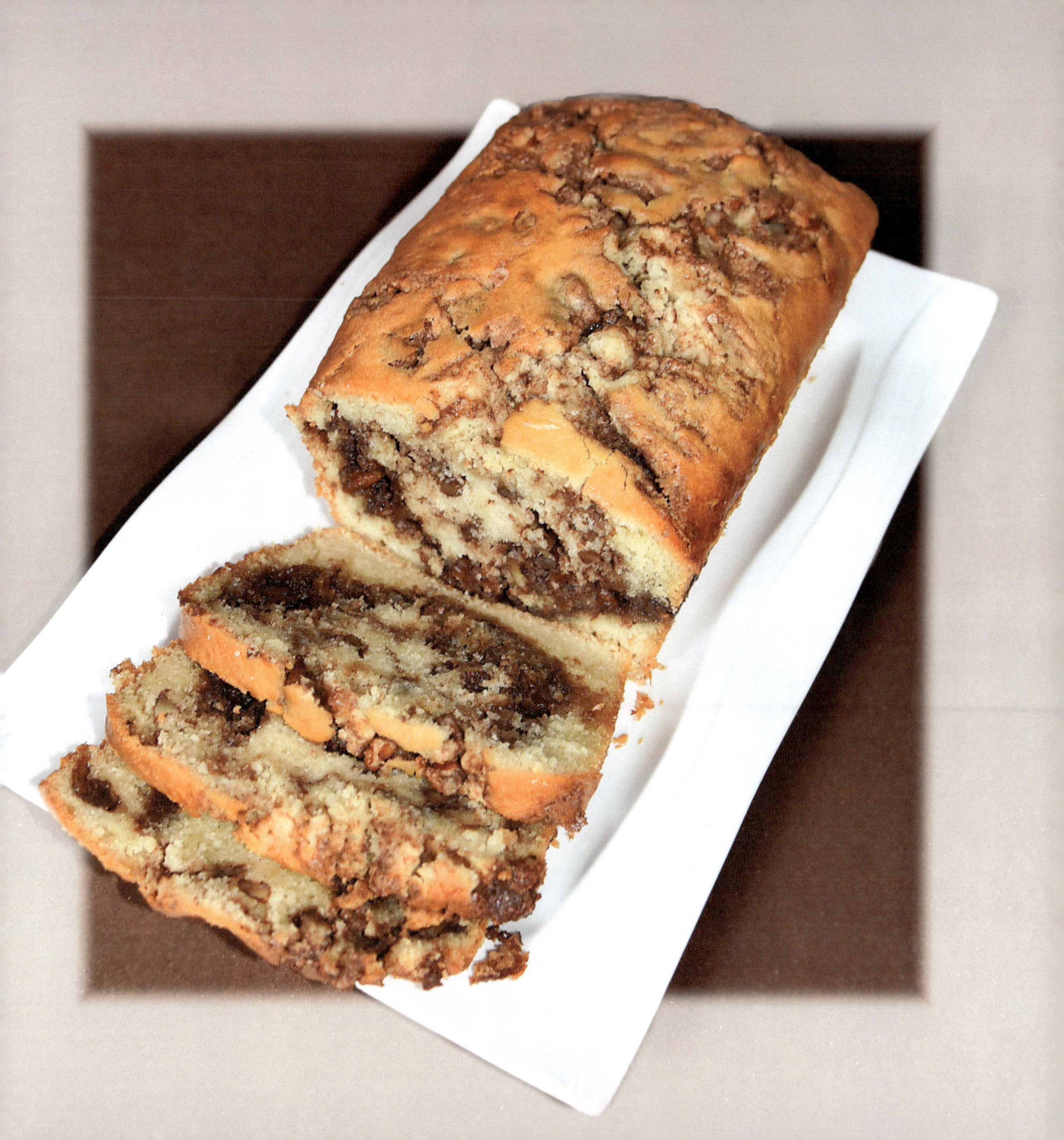

Pistachio Cake

Ingredients

150g (1¼ cup) shelled pistachios, plus 50g (½ cup) extra to decorate
180ml sunflower oil
180g (1 cup) caster sugar
3 large eggs
2 teaspoons vanilla extract
2 unwaxed lemons, zest only
150g (1¼ cup) plain flour
45g (½ cup) ground almonds
pinch salt
1½ teaspoons baking powder
1 teaspoon bicarbonate of soda
75g (¼ cup) soured cream

Topping

50g (½ cup) roasted pistachios
50g (¼ cup) caster sugar
juice of half lemon

Method

1. Preheat the oven to 180°C / gas 4 / 350°F
2. Line a 900g loaf tin with parchment paper
3. In a food processor, pulse 150g pistachios to make a powder.
4. In a large bowl, mix together the sunflower oil, caster sugar, eggs, vanilla extract, and lemon zest. Whisk until combined.
5. In a separate bowl, add the flour, ground pistachios, ground almonds, salt, baking powder and bicarbonate soda. Stir until well combined then fold into the wet ingredients in the other bowl.
6. Fold in the soured cream.
7. Pour the mixture into the prepared tin and bake for 20 minutes, then lower the oven to 150°C / Gas 2 / 300°F and bake for 1 hour or until a skewer inserted into the middle of the cake comes out clean.

Topping
Heat all the topping ingredients in a small saucepan on a low heat until the sugar is dissolved and slightly syrupy.
Drizzle over the cake and let it cool in the tin before removing.

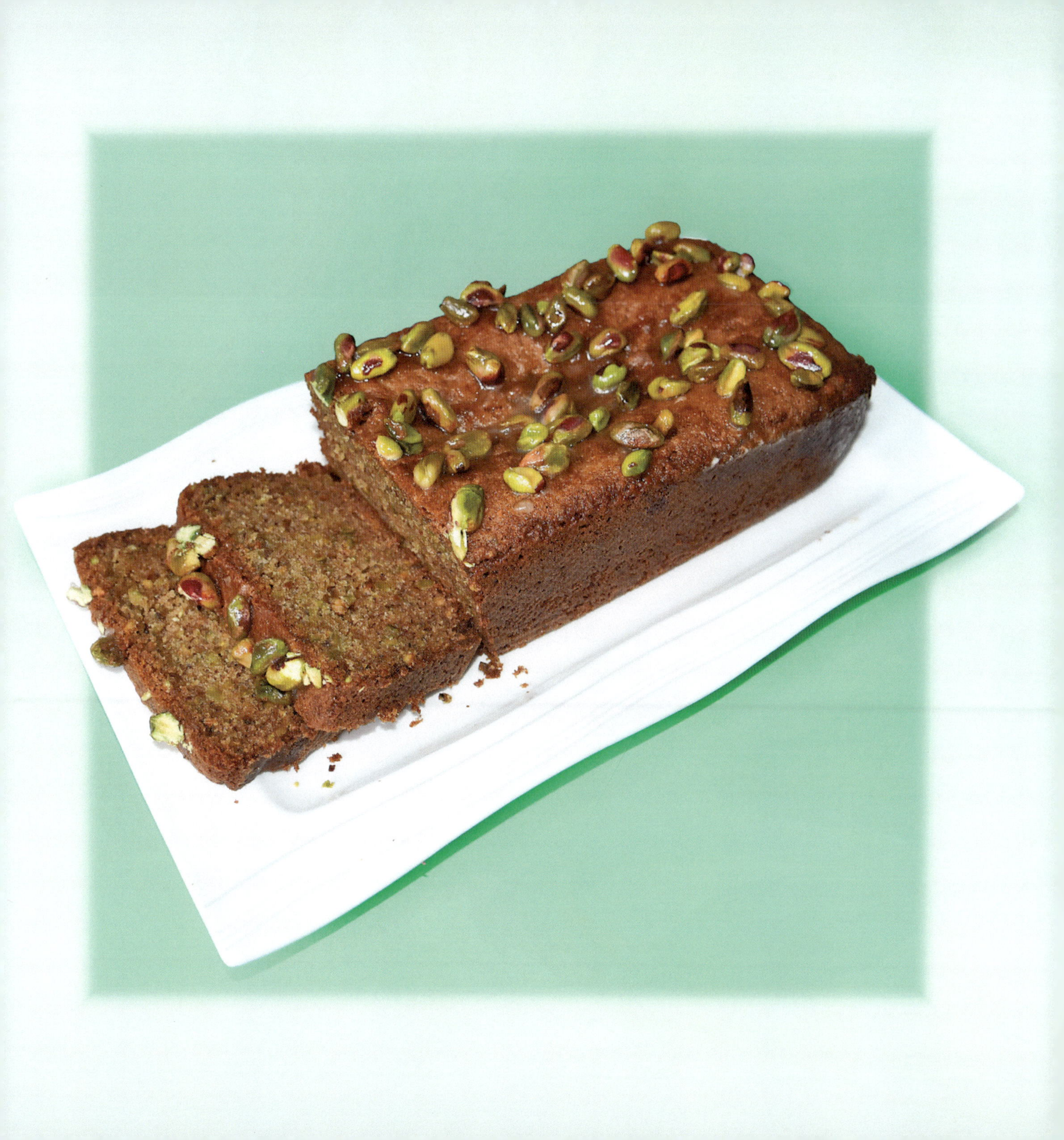

Plum & Custard Loaf Cake

Ingredients

225g (1 cup) salted butter, softened
225g (1 cup) light brown soft sugar
5 large eggs, lightly beaten
1 teaspoon vanilla extract
225g (1¾ cup) self-raising flour, sifted
75g (¾ cup) ground almonds
5 tablespoons custard powder
7 plums, stoned and chopped into small chunks
1 tablespoon flaked almonds

Method

1. Preheat the oven to 180°C / gas 4 / 350°F
2. Line a 900g loaf tin with parchment paper
3. In a bowl, beat together the butter and sugar with electric beaters, until light.
4. Gradually add the eggs, beating between each addition followed by the vanilla extract
5. Add the flour, ground almonds and custard powder to the mixture, folding with a large spoon to combine.
6. Fold through the chopped plums reserving a handful for the top.
7. Spoon the mixture into the prepared tin, scatter with the remaining plums and flaked almonds
8. Bake for 40 minutes then reduce the oven to 150°C / Gas 2 / 300°F and bake for a further 50 minutes or until a skewer inserted into the centre comes out clean.
9. Allow to cool in the tin for 10 minutes before removing to a wire rack to cool completely.

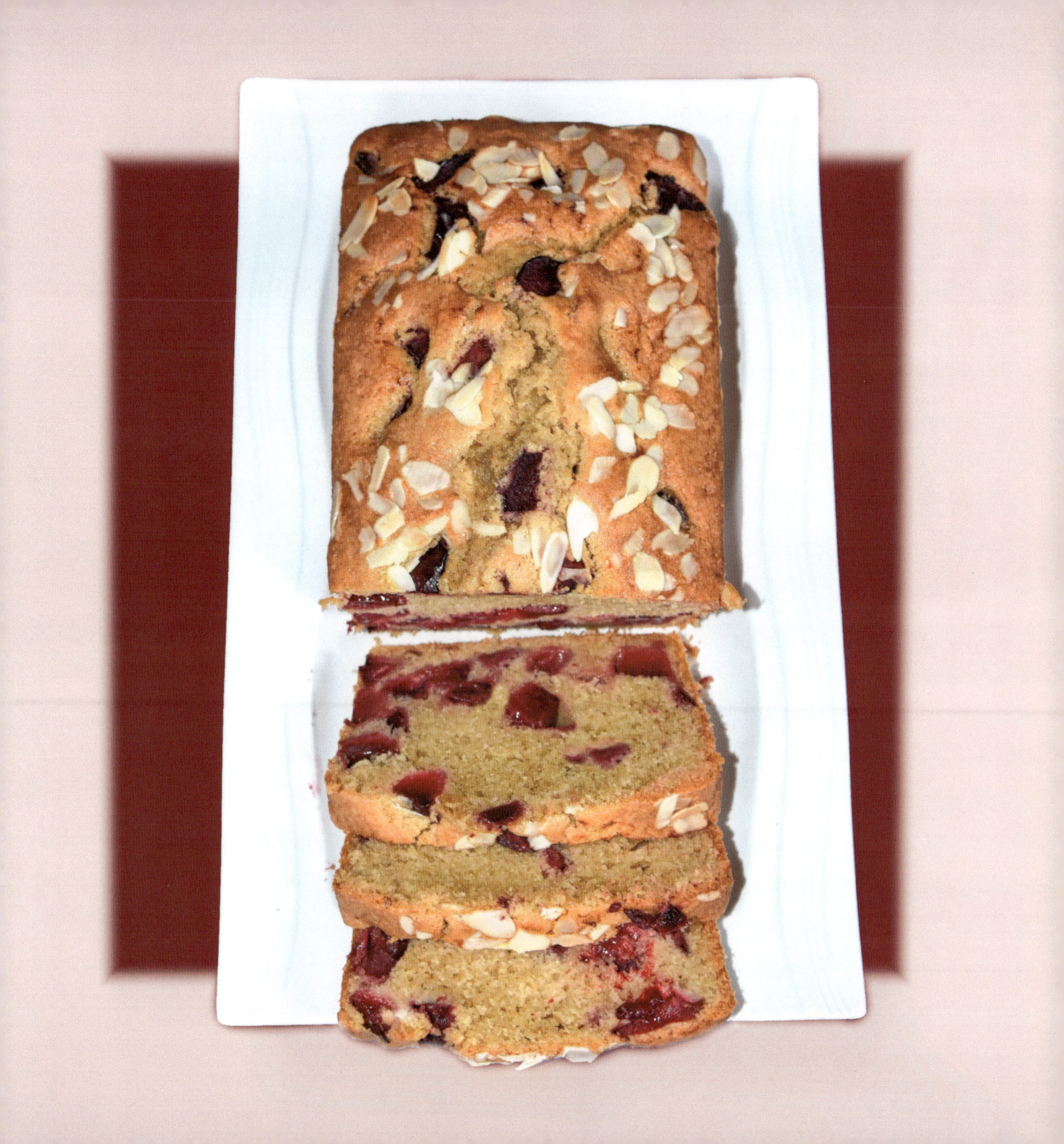

Raspberry White Chocolate Cake

Ingredients

285g (¼ cup) plain flour
200g (1 cup) caster sugar
½ teaspoons baking powder
½ teaspoon salt
280ml buttermilk
185ml vegetable oil (sunflower or rapeseed)
3 large eggs
2 teaspoons vanilla extract
100g (¾ cup) white chocolate
150g (1¼ cup) raspberries, fresh or frozen, gently tossed in 1 tablespoon flour

White Chocolate Drizzle

100g White Chocolate

Method

1. Preheat the oven to 170C / gas 3 / 325F
2. Line a 900g loaf tin with parchment paper
3. In a large bowl, mix together the flour, sugar, baking powder, and salt. Set aside.
4. In a separate bowl, whisk together the buttermilk, oil, eggs, and vanilla extract.
5. Slowly add the wet ingredients to the dry ingredients. Stir until combined.
6. Gently fold in the white chocolate and flour dusted raspberries.
7. Pour batter into prepared loaf pan
8. Bake for 90-100 minutes, or until a wood skewer comes out clean.
9. Leave to cool in the tin
10. Loosen the end sides of the loaf cake with a knife and place on a serving plate.

White Chocolate Drizzle

Melt the white chocolate in a small, microwave safe bowl. Heat for 30 seconds, stir, and heat for 30 more seconds. Stir until white chocolate is smooth. Drizzle the white chocolate glaze over the cooled loaf cake.
Leave the white chocolate to set

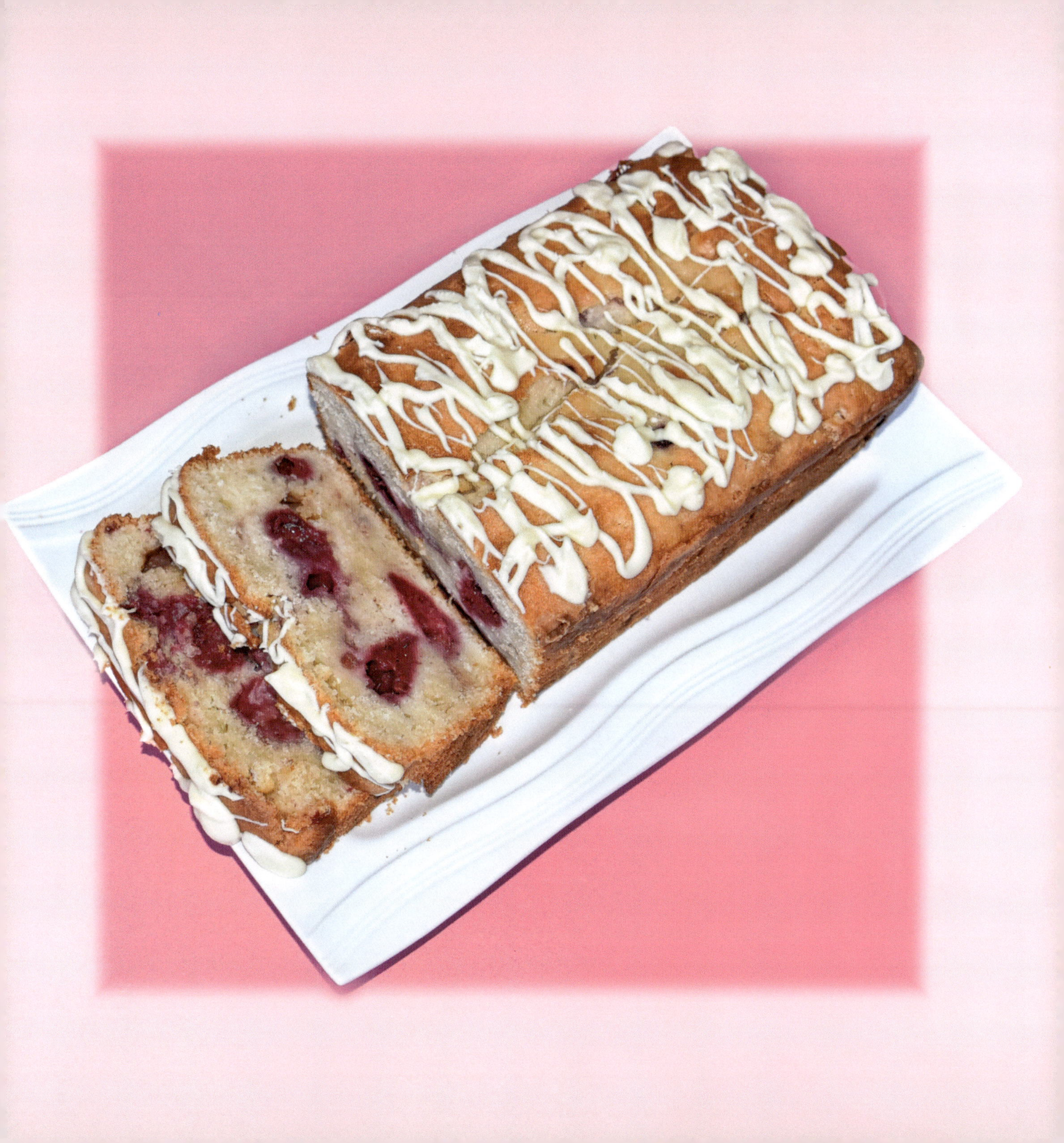

Red Velvet Cake

Ingredients

125g (½ cup) unsalted butter
250g (1¼ cup) caster Sugar
3 large eggs
35g (¼ cup) cocoa powder
1 teaspoon red food colouring
1 teaspoon vanilla extract
250ml buttermilk
300g (2½ cup) plain flour
1 teaspoon baking powder
1 teaspoon bicarbonate of soda
2 teaspoon white wine vinegar

Cream Cheese Frosting

125g (½ cup) unsalted butter (room temperature, use block butter, not a spread)
125g (1 cup) icing sugar
250g (1 cup) full-fat cream cheese
1 teaspoon vanilla extract

Cocoa for dusting (optional)

Method

1. Preheat the oven to 170C / gas 3 / 325F
2. Line a 900g loaf tin with parchment paper
3. Beat together the butter and caster sugar in a bowl until smooth.
4. Add in the eggs, cocoa powder, red food colouring and vanilla extract and beat until combined.
5. Add in the buttermilk and plain flour.
6. Beat in the baking powder, bicarbonate of soda and white wine vinegar.
7. Spoon the mixture into the loaf tin, and smooth over.
8. Bake for 60 minutes or until the middle of the cake comes out clean when poked with a skewer.
9. Leave to cool in the tin.

Cream Cheese Frosting

1. Beat the unsalted butter and sifted icing sugar together until light and fluffy.
2. Add in full-fat cream cheese (drain if needed), and the vanilla.
3. It should be a thick and smooth frosting once finished. If it turns too runny put in the fridge till it thickens up.

To Decorate

1. Cut the cake in half and sread with half the frosting and sandwich together
2. Spread the rest of the frosting on top of the cake and dust with the cocoa.

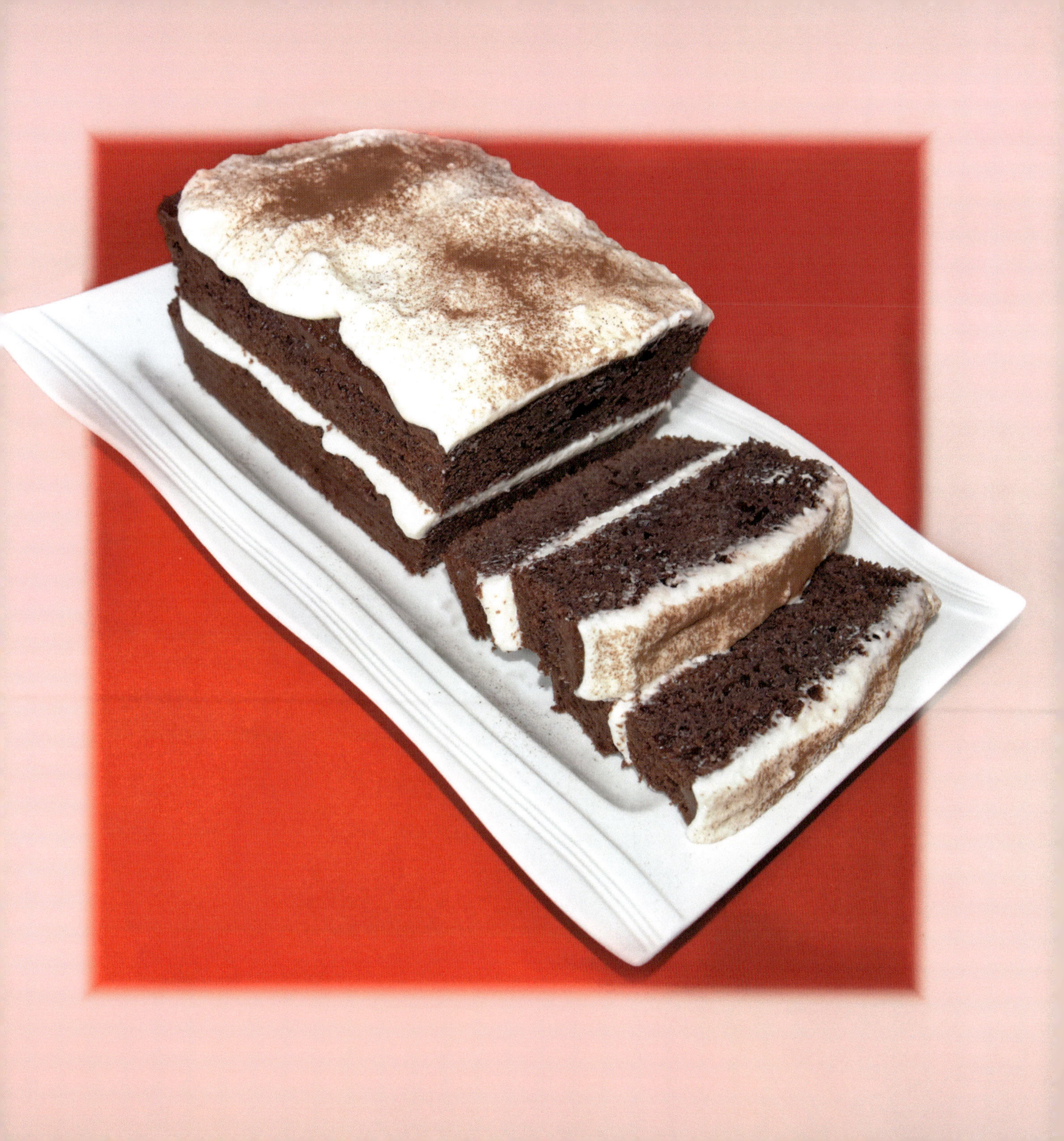

Sachertorte

Ingredients

140g (1 cup) dark chocolate, broken into pieces
140g (½ cup) unsalted butter, softened
100g (½ cup) caster sugar
1 teaspoon vanilla extract
5 large eggs, separated
85g (¾ cup) ground almonds
60g (½ cup) plain flour, sieved

Filling
300g (1 cup) apricot jam
2 tablespoon hot water

Chocolate Glaze
100g (¾ cup) dark chocolate
50g (¼ cup) caster sugar
35ml water

Decorations for cake (optional)

Method

1. Preheat the oven to 180°C / gas 4 / 350°F
2. Line a 900g loaf tin with parchment paper
3. Melt the chocolate in a microwave in 30 second bursts, stirring until melted. Set aside.
4. Beat the butter with the sugar until creamy.
5. Add the chocolate, vanilla, and egg yolks
6. Fold in the ground almonds and flour.
7. In a separate bowl, whisk the egg whites until they are stiff. Add about 1/3 to the chocolate mixture and stir. Gently fold in the remaining egg whites.
8. Pour the mixture into the prepared tin
9. Bake in the oven for 50 minutes, or until a skewer inserted into the middle comes out clean. Leave to cool in the tin.

Filling
Heat the apricot jam and water in a small pan, then press through a sieve.
Slice the cake into three layers and sandwich together with 2/3 of the apricot jam.
Spread the rest of the jam over the top and sides of the cake and leave to set.

Chocolate Glaze
Melt all the chocolate glaze ingredients together in a microwave in 30 second bursts, stirring to combine.
Let it cool down a little. Pour the glaze over the cake to cover it in a thick layer.

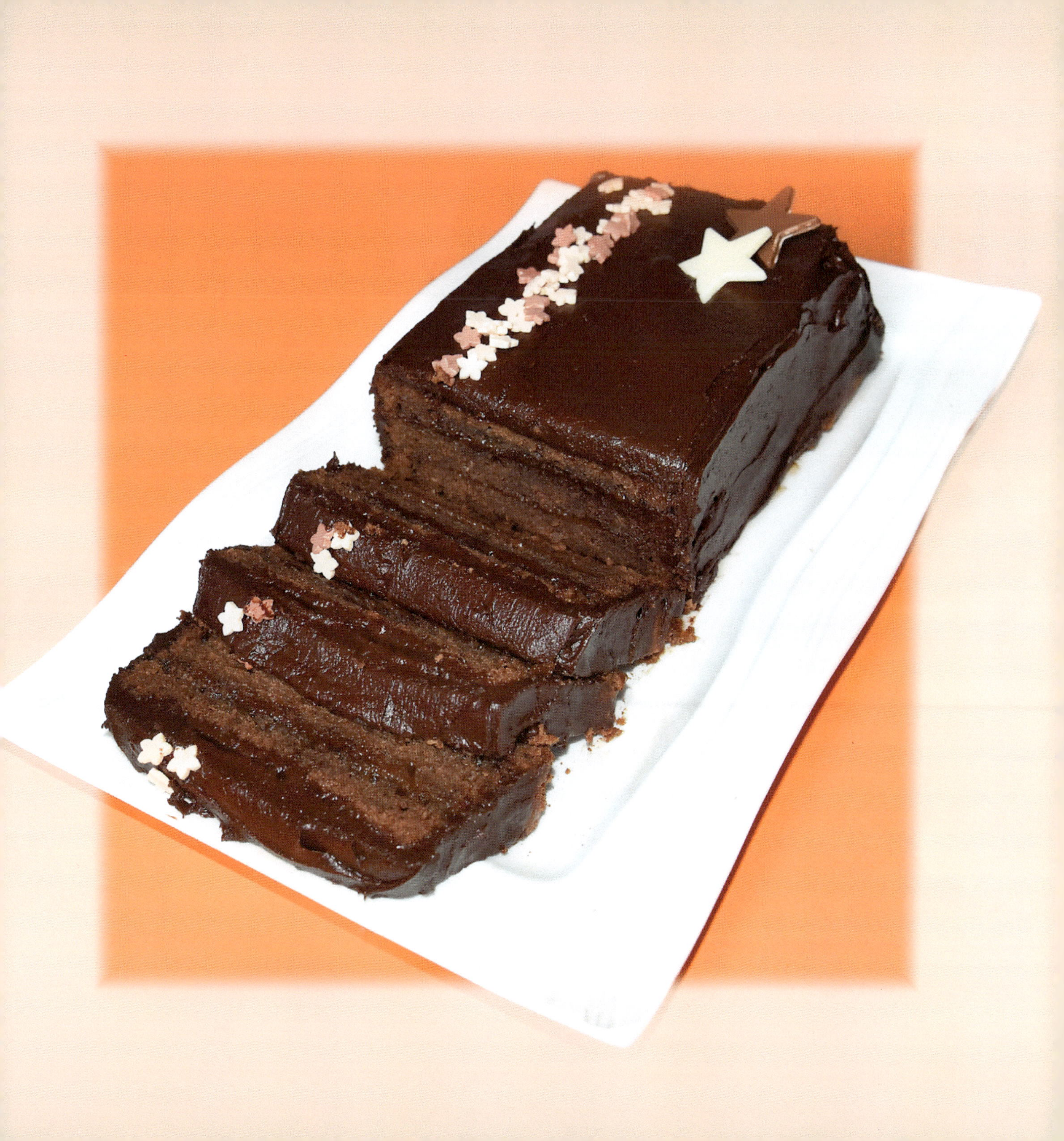

Simnel Loaf Cake

Ingredients

500g (2¼ cup) marzipan/almond paste
200g (1 cup) light muscovado sugar
300g (1¼ cup) butter
5 medium eggs
300g (2½ cup) self raising flour
250g (1¼ cup) mixed dried fruit
2 lemons, zested and juiced
2 tablespoons apricot jam

A ribbon for decoration (optional)

Method

1. Preheat the oven to 180°C / gas 4 / 350°F
2. Line a 900g loaf tin with parchment paper
3. Beat the butter and sugar together till pale and creamy.
4. Add the eggs one at a time
5. Fold in the flour, mixed fruit, lemon juice, zest.
6. Pour half the mixture into the loaf tin.
7. Chop 160g of the marzipan into small cubes and sprinkle half over the mixture in the tin.
8. Top with some more mixture, then the rest of the chopped marzipan and then finish off with the remaining mixture.
9. Bake in the oven for 50 minutes then reduce the oven to 150°C / Gas 2 / 300°F and bake for a further 40 minutes till a skewer inserted into the middle of the cake comes out clean.
10. Allow to cool in the tin.
11. Use some of the remaining marzipan to make 11 small balls and set aside.
12. Dust a worktop with icing sugar and roll out the left over marzipan to a rectangle the size of the top of the cake.
13. Heat the apricot jam in a saucepan or microwave to loosen, then brush the top of the cake and cover with the rolled out marzipan.
14. Dip the bottom of the marzipan balls into the apricot jam and arrange on top of the cake.
15. Preheat the grill and put the cake under it till the marzipan has browned.

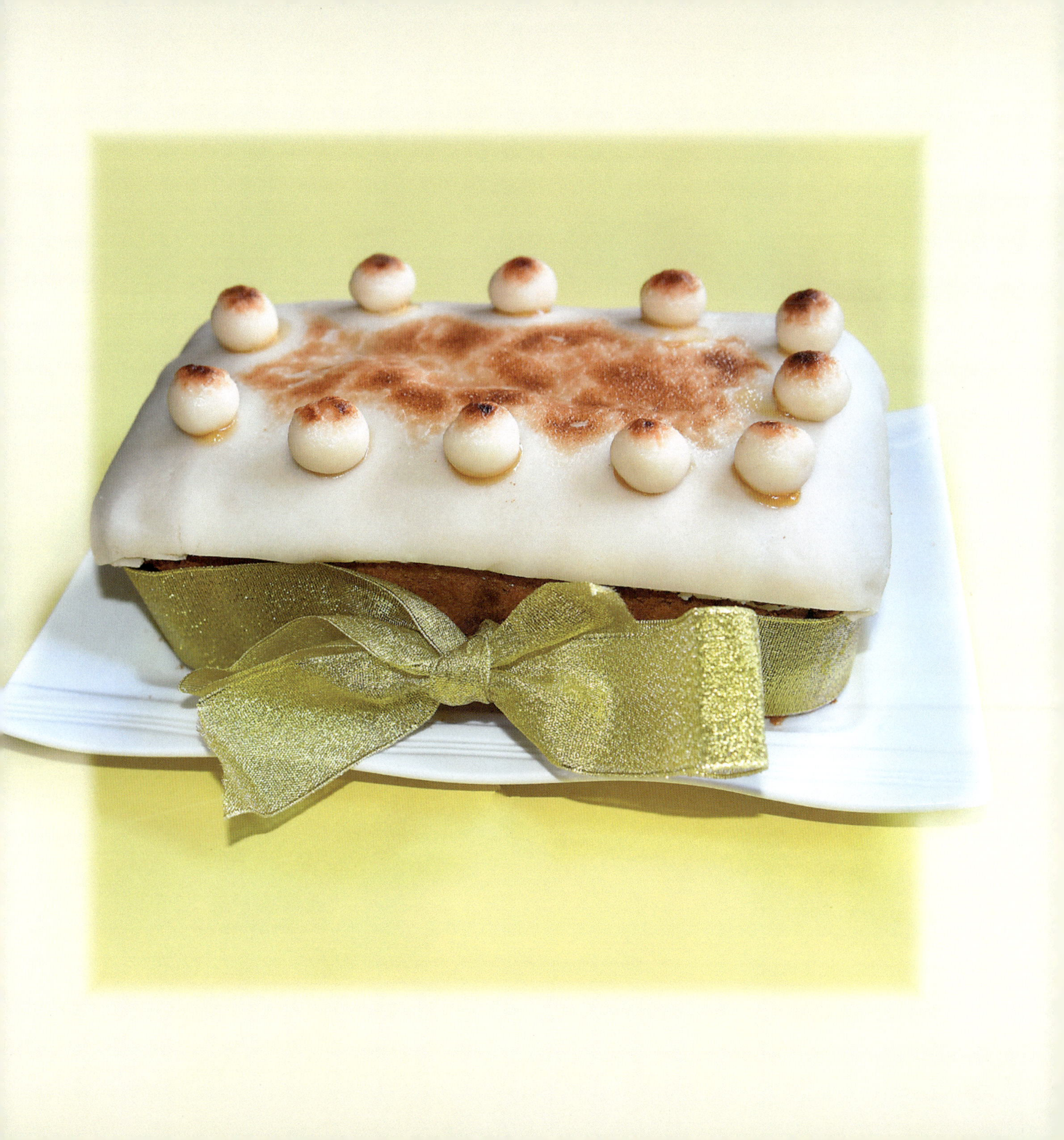

Stem Ginger Cake

Ingredients

150g (¾ cup) unsalted Butter
150ml single cream
130g (½ cup) dark brown soft sugar
150g (½ cup) golden syrup
130g (½ cup) treacle
3 large eggs
300g (2½ cup) plain flour
1½ teaspoons baking powder
2 tablespoons ground ginger
2 teaspoons ground cinnamon
4 knobs stem ginger in syrup roughly chopped

Method

1. Preheat the oven to 180°C / gas 4 / 350°F
2. Line a 900g loaf tin with parchment paper
3. Put the butter, cream, sugar, golden syrup and treacle in a saucepan and melt over a gentle heat until the sugar is dissolved.
4. Pour this mixture into a bowl and cool for 5 minutes.
5. Then whisk in the eggs.
6. In a separate bowl measure out the flour, baking powder, ground ginger and cinnamon then whisk into the liquid mixture.
7. Stir through half the stem ginger.
8. Tip into the cake tin and scatter the remaining stem ginger on the top.
9. Bake for 30 minutes then turn the oven down to 150°C / Gas 2 / 300°F and bake for a further 60 minutes. until a skewer inserted into the centre comes out clean.
10. Allow the cake to cool in the tin before turning out.

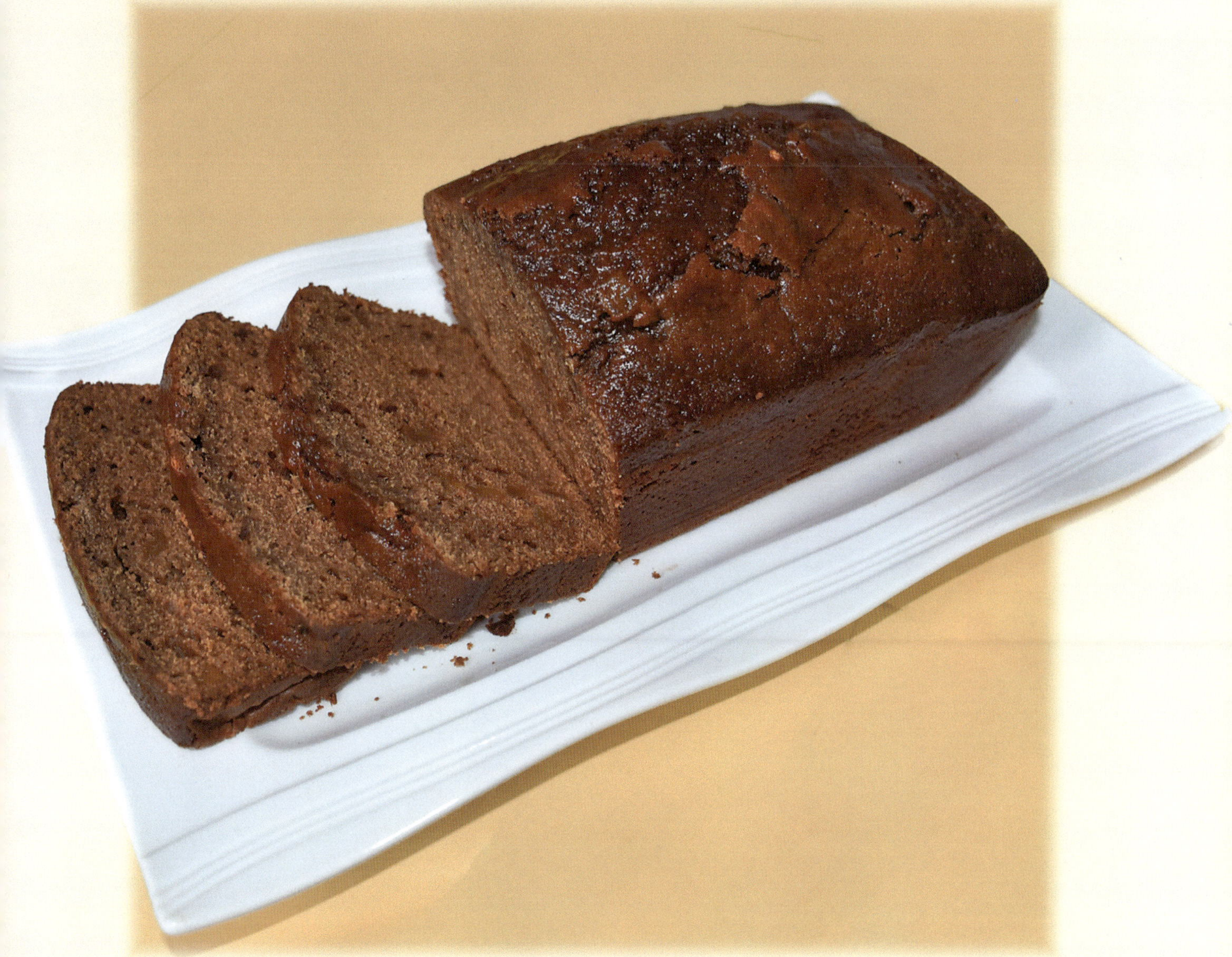

Toffee Apple Cake

Ingredients

450g (3½ cup) self raising flour
2 teaspoons baking powder
1 teaspoon mixed spice
250g (1 cup) cold butter, diced
2 medium Bramley apples, peeled cored and diced into 1cm pieces
250g (1¼ cup) light muscovado sugar
4 medium eggs, beaten
2 teaspoons Caramel or Toffee flavouring (optional)

Demerara sugar for sprinkling on top

Method

1. Preheat the oven to 190°C / gas 5 / 375°F
2. Line a 900g loaf tin with parchment paper.
3. Sift the flour, baking powder and mixed spice into a large bowl. Rub in the diced butter to form fine breadcrumbs.
4. Stir in the diced apple and sugar.
5. Then gradually stir in the beaten eggs, and flavouring to form a stiff mixture.
6. Spoon into the prepared tin and level the surface with the back of a spoon. Sprinkle some demerara sugar on top.
7. Bake for 30 minutes then reduce the oven to 150°C / Gas 2 / 300°F and bake for a further 75 minutes until springy to the touch and a skewer inserted into the middle comes out clean
8. Leave to cool in the tin before turning out on to a plate.

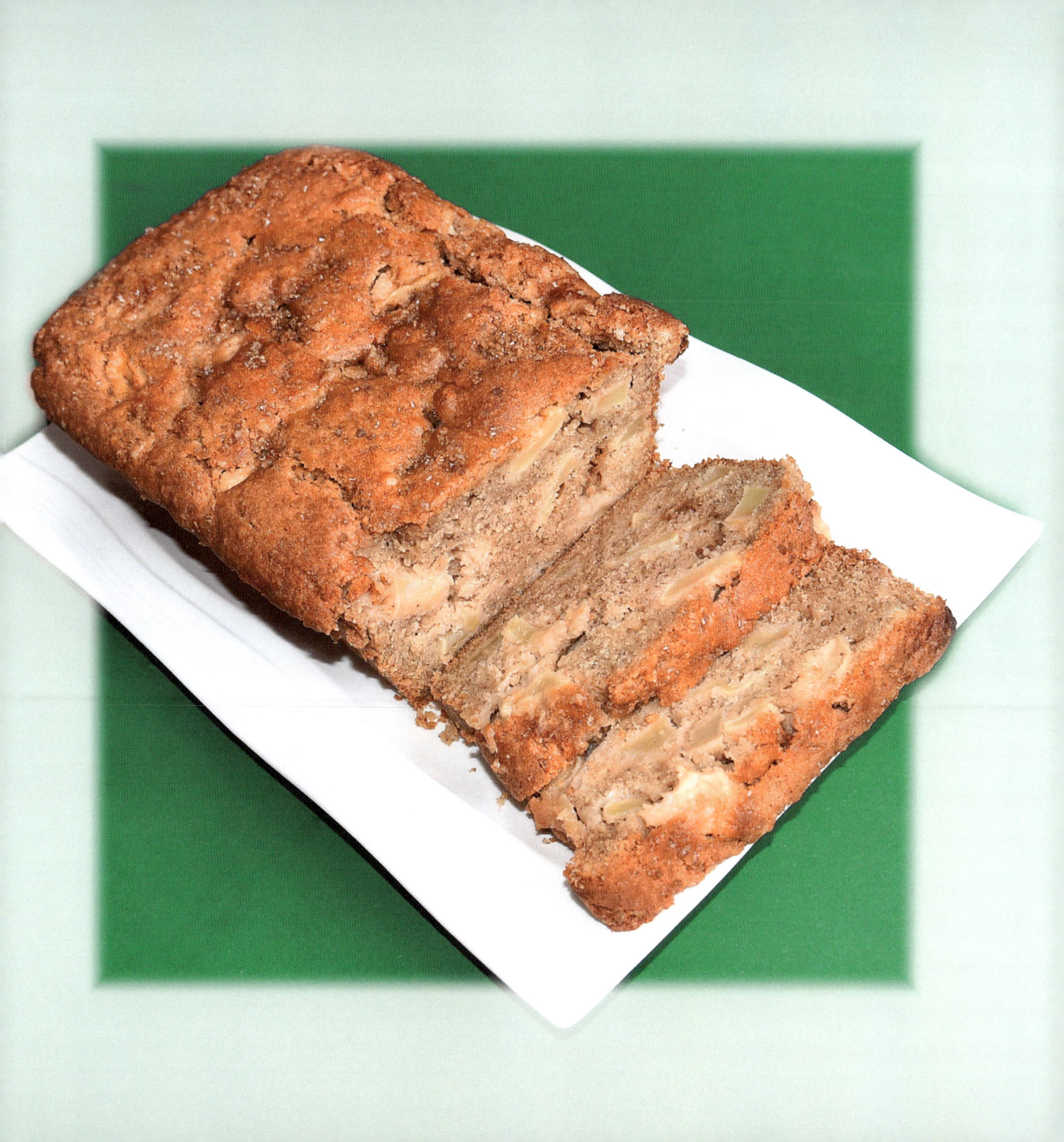

Victoria Sponge

Ingredients

250g (1 cup) unsalted butter
250g (1¼ cup) caster sugar
4 medium eggs
250g (2 cups) self raising flour
1 teaspoon vanilla extract
1-2 tablespoons milk

Buttercream Filling
125g (½ cup) unsalted butter
125g (1 cup) icing sugar
1 teaspoon vanilla extract
4 tablespoons raspberry or blackberry jam, stirred to soften

Method

1. Preheat the oven to 180°C / gas 4 / 350°F
2. Line a 900g loaf tin with parchment paper.
3. Place the butter and sugar in a bowl and beat together until pale and creamy.
3. Add the eggs one at a time beating after each one, then add the vanilla extract.
4. Fold in the flour in two additions
5. Mix in the milk to bring the mixture to a dropping consistency.
6. Pour into the prepared tin.
7. Place in the oven for 50 minutes then reduce the oven to 150°C / Gas 2 / 300°F and bake for another 25 minutes until a skewer inserted in the middle of the cake comes out clean.
8. Leave to cool in the tin then turn out on a plate.
9. Slice the cake horizontally in half.

Filling
Put the butter in a bowl and beat until fluffy. Add sifted icing sugar and lightly beat in. Mix in the vanilla.

Spread the buttercream over the bottom sponge, spoon over the jam and cover with the top half of the sponge.

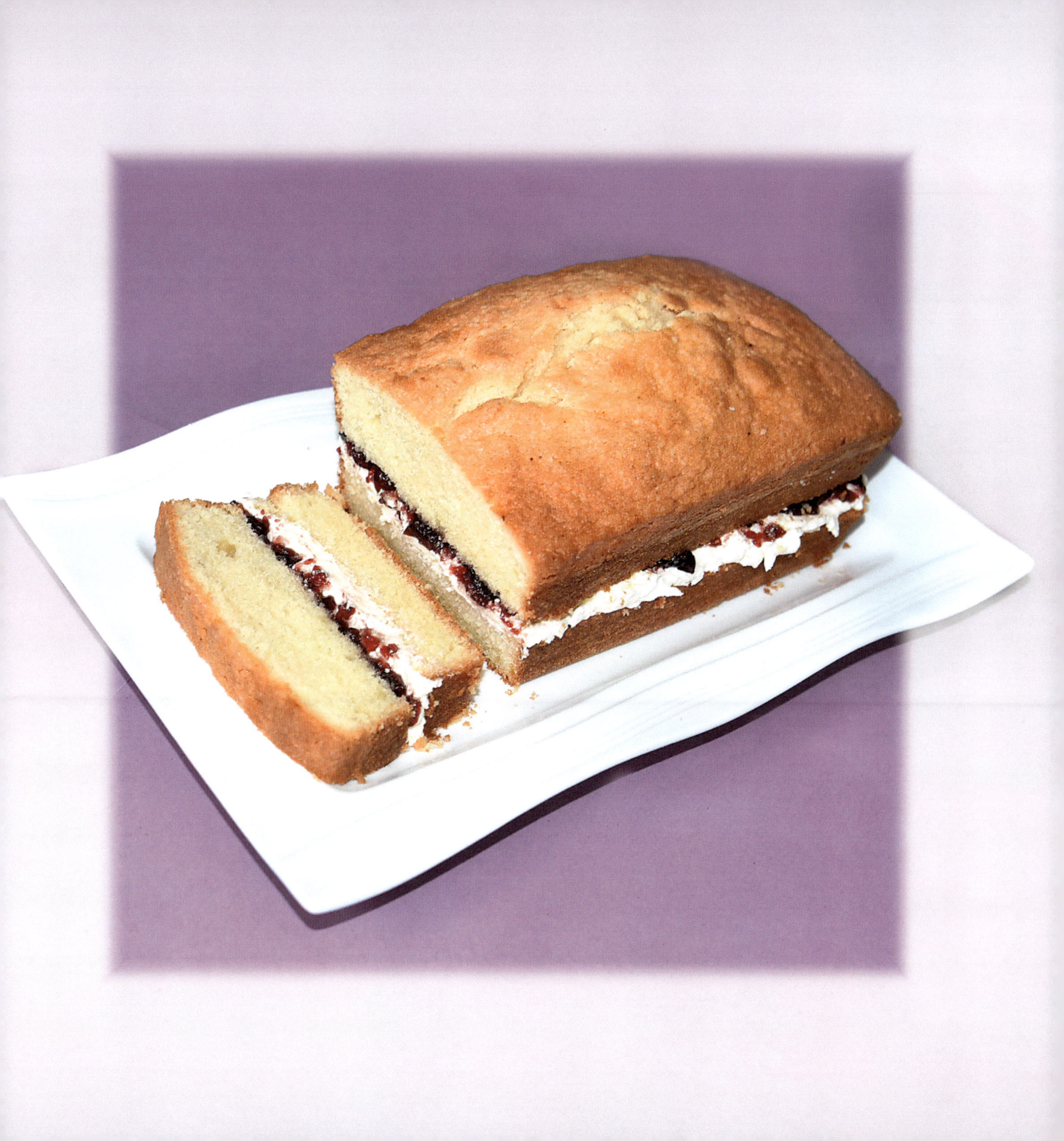

Printed in Great Britain
by Amazon